ARSENAL

Bill Day

Illustrated by Craig Warwick

Purnell

A PURNELL BOOK
Text © Bill Day 1988
Illustrations © Macdonald & Co (Publishers) Ltd 1988
First published in Great Britain in 1988
by Macdonald & Co (Publishers) Ltd
London & Sydney
A member of Maxwell Pergamon Publishing Corporation plc

Macdonald & Co (Publishers) Ltd
Greater London House
Hampstead Road
London NW1 7QX

British Library Cataloguing in Publication Data

Day, Bill
    Arsenal. – (Football clubs).
    1. England. Association football. Clubs.
    Arsenal Football Club, history
    I. Title II. Series
    796.334'63'0942143

ISBN 0-361 08356-4
ISBN 0-361-08357-2 Pbk

Cover photograph: Sporting Pictures (UK) Ltd

Typeset, printed and bound in Great Britain by
Hazell Watson & Viney Limited
Member of BPCC plc
Aylesbury, Bucks, England

Contents

Useful Addresses

Arsenal Football Club: Arsenal Stadium,
Avenell Road, Highbury, London N5 1BU.

Supporters' Club Information: Administrator:
Barry Baker c/o 154 St Thomas's Road, Finsbury Park,
London N4.

There are many regional branches of the Supporters' Club.
Write to the above person for details of the one nearest to
you.

Arsenal Honours

First Division Champions: 1931, 33, 34, 35, 38, 48, 53, 71

F.A. Cup Winners: 1930, 36, 50, 71, 79

Littlewoods Cup Winners: 1987

European Fairs Cup Winners: 1970

(Arsenal hold the record for the longest unbroken run in
Division One)

ARSENAL 1987–88 LEAGUE RECORD

Match	Date	Venue	Opponents	Result		Goalscorers
1	Aug 15	H	Liverpool	L	1–2	Davis
2	19	A	Manchester U	D	0–0	
3	22	A	QPR	L	0–2	
4	29	H	Portsmouth	W	6–0	Smith 3, Rocastle, Adams, Davis
5	31	A	Luton T	D	1–1	Davis
6	Sept 12	A	Nottingham F	W	1–0	Smith
7	19	H	Wimbledon	W	3–0	Thomas (pen), Smith, Thorn (og)
8	26	H	West Ham U	W	1–0	Sansom
9	Oct 3	H	Charlton Ath	W	3–0	Groves, Thomas, Adams
10	10	H	Oxford U	W	2–0	Davis, Williams
11	18	A	Tottenham H	W	2–1	Rocastle, Thomas
12	24	H	Derby Co	W	2–1	Richardson, Thomas (pen)
13	31	A	Newcastle U	W	1–0	Smith
14	Nov 3	H	Chelsea	W	3–1	Richardson 2, Wegerle (og)
15	14	A	Norwich C	W	4–2	Rocastle 2, Thomas, Groves
16	21	A	Southampton	L	0–1	
17	28	A	Watford	L	0–2	
18	Dec 5	H	Sheffield W	W	3–1	Richardson, Groves, Merson
19	13	A	Coventry C	D	0–0	
20	19	H	Everton	D	1–1	Rocastle
21	26	H	Nottingham F	L	0–2	
22	28	A	Wimbledon	L	1–3	Quinn
23	Jan 1	A	Portsmouth	D	1–1	Smith
24	2	H	QPR	D	0–0	
25	16	A	Liverpool	L	0–2	
26	24	H	Manchester U	L	1–2	Quinn
27	Feb 13	H	Luton T	W	2–1	Thomas, Rocastle
28	27	H	Charlton Ath	W	4–0	Merson 2, Thomas, Smith
29	Mar 6	H	Tottenham H	W	2–1	Smith, Groves
30	19	H	Newcastle U	D	1–1	Groves
31	26	A	Derby Co	D	0–0	
32	30	A	Oxford	D	0–0	
33	Apr 2	A	Chelsea	D	1–1	McLaughlin (og)
33	4	H	Norwich	W	2–0	Smith, Groves
34	9	A	Southampton	L	2–4	Bond (og), Davis
35	12	A	West Ham	W	1–0	Thomas
36	15	H	Watford	L	0–1	
37	30	A	Sheffield W	D	3–3	Merson (2), Smith
38	May 2	H	Coventry	D	1–1	Marwood (pen)
39	7	A	Everton	W	2–1	Thomas, Hayes

Final League position: 6th

Introduction

HOW did a works' football team without kit rise from kicking a football about on common land in the suburbs of South London, to a position of standing among the world's elite League clubs? This book will tell you. It charts Arsenal Football Club's early struggle for survival; the big move to the showpiece Highbury Stadium; and its unprecedented success under Herbert Chapman, the giant manager of his era between two world wars. It describes the Tom Whittaker Years of post-War triumph when a spindly-legged captain named Joe Mercer proved a professional footballer could fill his sideboard with trophies and mementoes – and still play for fun. It records how England's golden boy Billy Wright failed to find the success at managerial level he had enjoyed playing for his country; the glorious Double-winning feat of Bertie Mee's heroic Arsenal; stirring Cup-winning exploits and a baptism of fire in Europe under Terry Neill; and the rampant success of George Graham's young lions who roared to success in the Littlewoods Cup.

Above all, this book is about players, great players from Charlie Buchan to Charlie Nicholas; from the sorcery of Alex James to the explosive talent of David Rocastle; from England's dynamic defender Eddie Hapgood to World Cup campaigner Kenny Sansom; from goal-grabbing Ted Drake to thunderboots Malcolm 'Supermac' Macdonald; from wizard winger Cliff Bastin to Liam Brady, Charlie George, Alan Ball, David O'Leary, Tony Adams . . . and a host of other golden Gunners.

It is a story of the happiness and heartache, triumph and disaster, and all the tears and the joy that go towards making Arsenal Football Club a by-word wherever and whenever the game of football is discussed.

Chapter One

Early Days

THE very name 'Arsenal' carries a special ring of magic whenever it crops up in a discussion about football.

Of the 92 Football League clubs, only Aldershot gains preference alphabetically over Arsenal. But as Aldershot have never occupied a position higher than the Third Division, Arsenal, of the First Division, is the first club to be published in the programme of fixtures for Saturday games, and the first result to be given when the majority of punters check their coupons on a Saturday night and say: 'It's not my turn to win a million pounds this week.'

Arsenal's place in history as the 'number one' League club was established as far back as 1919 when it rose to the First Division, where it has now been, without interruption for more than 60 years. Not even Liverpool, Manchester United, Everton or Arsenal's great North London rivals Tottenham Hotspur, can match them for this remarkable run among the Football League's elite clubs.

All work and no play . . .

Proud Arsenal have enjoyed high ideals since they decided to call themselves Royal Arsenal way back in 1886, the year of their formation. The Arsenal story begins when a group of men in a government-run munitions factory at Woolwich in Kent, caught the national fervour for recreation. Long, hard shifts in the foundry encouraged the men to think that there was more to life than work. They wanted to play some sort of sport in their spare time. Cricket and rugby were big in Kent, but the growing sport for working class lads in Victorian times was football.

A soccer-loving Scot named David Danskin decided to start a works football team, and no sooner had he persuaded the players of the factory's Dial Square workshop to have a whip-round to buy a football than two Nottingham Forest players, Morris Bates and Fred Beardsley, arrived to work at the factory.

Beardsley, a goalkeeper, was a football nut. He had been sacked from jobs for taking too much time off to play football, but if he tended to upset shop floor foremen over his enthusiasm for the game, the new club was only too happy for his support.

Dial Square's first game was against a team called Eastern Wanderers. The historic match was played on 11 December 1886 when the factory team crossed the River Thames to play the game on the Isle of Dogs. The pitch bore no comparison to the handsome, manicured grass of Arsenal's famous Highbury stadium today. There were no crossbars, hardly any pitch markings, and players spent most of the match

trespassing in back gardens to retrieve the ball or
risking their health – and lives – in fishing the ball
from a stinking sewer that ran the length of one
side of the pitch.

Dial Square, 6–0 winners that day, were worth
better than this, and on Christmas Day that year
David Danskin called a meeting in a Woolwich
pub to officially form a club called Royal Arsenal.

Goalkeepers wore the same colour shirts as out-
field players in those days, and Fred Beardsley's
red Forest shirt was so admired by Royal Arsenal
that he wrote to his old club to see whether they
could supply his new team with a set of their old
kit. Almost by return of post, Beardsley received
a set of immaculately pressed red shirts, a football, and a message wishing him good luck in his
future.

Arsenal have worn red and white ever since,
the white being added in 1933 before a match
against Liverpool.

A humble Jubilee
Royal Arsenal used part of Plumstead Common
as their home ground. Stones lying on the surface
of the pitch could cut a player's legs to ribbons.
Deep ruts could rupture ankles. The common
was used for exercising dogs, and in midweek
it echoed to the urgent thud of horses' hooves
carrying the Royal Horse Artillery through the
morning mists of Victorian England.

Royal Arsenal's first fixture was against Erith
on 8 January 1887, the year in which Queen Vic-
toria enjoyed her Jubilee celebrations.

Nothing so grand for Royal Arsenal! The team
carried the goalposts from Beardsley's back

11

garden for the first match on the Common. Former Forest stars Beardsley and Bates, a powerful header, were outstanding in a team that carved eight victories in 10 matches that first season. Danskin was also a leading member of that inaugural side, and several fellow Scots were drafted in to make the club one of the strongest in the region.

Going professional

Arsenal won the Kent Senior Cup and the London Charity cup in 1890, and the London Cup in 1891.

By now they had moved from the public parkland at Plumstead Common to the Manor Ground in Plumstead, a pitch that was to remain their home for the next 20 years and attract huge crowds.

Now called Woolwich Arsenal, the team were elected to the Football League's Second Division in 1893, and so became London's first League club.

Seven clubs were elected to the Football League in that golden summer of 1893, among them Liverpool and Newcastle United who, with Arsenal, were to carve such illustrious futures for themselves in what was destined to become 'the greatest League in the world'.

Newcastle were Woolwich Arsenal's first League opponents. Their defence was cracked twice by Shaw and Elliott, but they popped in two goals to share the points on that memorable day in early September 1893.

Woolwich Arsenal made an unspectacular start to life as a professional club. They found it hard to complete the transition from being a small works' team with fairly narrow horizons to being a major professional club, paying wages, charging gate receipts, and organising long journeys to away matches in the great football heartlands of the North.

The arrival of manager Harry Bradshaw in 1901 resulted in an immediate improvement in Arsenal's results in Division Two. Under his guidance, they came fourth in his first season, third in his second, and rose to second to win promotion to the First Division in 1904.

Arsenal's remarkable record is such that with the exception of two seasons, 1913–14 and 1914–15, they have remained members of the First Division ever since.

Goal-scoring days

Arsenal were almost unbeatable at home in that promotion-winning season of 1903–04, scoring 67 goals and letting in only five. The famous Preston North End were Champions that season, with a club by the name of Manchester United finishing third.

Jimmy Ashcroft played every match in that promotion year, and the team included Tommy Shanks, one of the great goal-scorers of that era with 25 strikes in League matches.

Another outstanding goal-scorer was about to join the club. His name was Andy Ducat, who crowned a remarkable début on Christmas Day 1905 by scoring a hat-trick against Newcastle. He went on to become an England international and became a double international when chosen to play cricket for his country.

Phil Kelso, a tough Scot, took over from Bradshaw with immediate results when regular home gates of 10,000 saw the club reach the F.A. Cup semi-finals in 1906, only for them to lose to their arch-enemies Newcastle.

But they cruised into the semi-finals the following season, losing to Sheffield Wednesday when goalkeeper Ashcroft was seriously injured. Those were the days before substitutes.

Bankruptcy blues
Occasional rushes of Cup success amidst mediocre performances in the League could not disguise the fact that, as a business, Woolwich Arsenal was a disaster.

The club's finances were in a desperate state, and the club's confidence was shaken further when Kelso resigned five years after his appointment. He followed in Bradshaw's footsteps to Fulham. (Fulham were to feed off Arsenal for managers over the next few decades.)

New manager George Morrell hardly stood a chance of success when he arrived in September 1908. He had no money to recruit, and so had to wield the axe, selling most of the big names.

Bankrupt, close to withdrawal from the League, and losing support at the gates, Woolwich Arsenal was ripe for take-over.

It was during the height of this period of alarm and fear for the future that Henry Norris, the power behind Fulham Football Club, emerged as the saviour of the club – despite the fact that for years he had helped fleece Arsenal of players. His popularity in North Kent was nil; but in 1910 he gained full control of the club, a move which

14

assured the club's future even if his enemies within had to force a welcoming smile.

His burning ambition was to build a club capable of competing against the might of the great Northern soccer playing areas; but he found himself in charge of a club that was destined for relegation.

Woolwich Arsenal won only one League game at home in 1912–13, still a record for any Football League club. At the end of the season they were reported to have assets totalling a meagre £19, but despite this grim adversity there was hope for a bright new future – at a new home.

At a special meeting of the League Management Committee, the club bid to move to a new ground in North London, known as Highbury.

Not the Milk Cup!
The first game at Highbury was staged on 6 September 1913 when the 'Woolwich' in their name was dropped, and plain Arsenal met Leicester Fosse in the Second Division, the game ending in a 2–1 victory for the Reds.

Scottish striker Andy Devine had the honour of scoring the first goal, but his team-mate George Jobey was to go down in football books for a homely episode that puts the players of those days in another world from 'millionaire' superstars of today's game. Jobey, injured in the game, was taken to his lodgings by milk cart during the game, as there were no dressing rooms.

Arsenal in the wars
A year later, in 1914, Europe was at war, and many Arsenal players and backroom staff were

tied up in the bloody conflict that was to last for the next four years.

The war had a devastating effect upon Arsenal. They lost players, they lost supporters, and at the end of the 1914–15 season, manager George Morrell was sacked to save money.

Rivalry on the pitch

By the end of the War Norris was counting the cost of a disastrous five year reign as Chairman, with the club £60,000 overdrawn.

The desperation of the situation called for desperate measures from Sir Henry Norris – he had been knighted in 1917 – and he embarked on a canvassing campaign that persuaded the Football League to grant Arsenal First Division status when the war ended. The decision was to infuriate deadly North London rivals Spurs.

In September 1922 the boardroom unrest between the two clubs spilled on to the pitch when two players were sent off in the North London derby. In the 1927–28 season all the bitterness was fanned again when Arsenal were accused of 'throwing' games to ensure that Spurs were relegated.

Post-war problems

Post-war Arsenal was managed by Leslie Knighton, a veteran of management at Huddersfield and Manchester City, who received the shock of his life when he studied Norris's instructions on how to run the playing side of the club.

His commandments read: 'You must not sign players under the height of 5ft 8ins; you must encourage local talent; you must not spend more

16

than £1,000 on players; you must not run a scouting system'!

In the next six years Arsenal were to enjoy only one season when they won more games than they lost in a League campaign.

The team takes the medicine

Arsenal were the focus of as much attention in the early 1920s as they are in more modern times. Before one important Cup match against West Ham, the struggling Knighton was approached by a Harley Street doctor to administer a 'courage' pill to each of his players.

'They do no harm, but tone up the nerves to produce maximum effort' claimed the doctor. Knighton, by now desperate for success, decided to pin his faith in the pills against a backcloth of scepticism by the team.

Knighton himself swallowed the first tablet to reassure the players. At 2.30 p.m. on match day they had all taken their tablets. At 2.50 p.m., the referee burst into the Arsenal dressing room to make a dramatic announcement: 'Gentlemen, the match is off because of fog.'

New management

Leslie Knighton's reign as manager ended just before the end of the 1924–25 season. Norris's ruthless dismissal of the Arsenal boss was to cost Knighton dearly, for he had been promised a benefit the following season.

On 11 May 1925, the *Athletic News* carried the following advertisement: 'Arsenal Football Club is open to receive applications for the position of team manager . . .' The advert went on to warn off managers who relied upon wheeling and dealing in the transfer market for success.

But Sir Henry Norris already knew the manager he wanted. He looked no further than Huddersfield and their brilliant team boss Herbert Chapman.

Chapter Two

Chapman Reigns Supreme

HERBERT CHAPMAN achieved the near impossible when he left Huddersfield Town to take charge at Arsenal at the end of the 1924–25 season. Fortified by F.A. Cup triumph and two straight Championships at Leeds Road, he transformed Arsenal over the next decade into a club whose very mention would gain instant recognition and approval across the great soccer-playing continents of the globe. Quite simply, Arsenal, in those days, were the greatest football club in the world.

The super-manager

Herbert Chapman was a Matt Busby, Bill Shankly, Bobby Robson, Brian Clough, rolled-into-one super manager! In those elegant and sophisticated days of the golden thirties, Chapman was to have more influence on the Football League and the way the game developed in England than any other manager before or since.

A Yorkshireman, who played for Spurs before moving into management at Northampton, Leeds, Huddersfield and then Arsenal, Herbert

Herbert Chapman, manager from 1925 to 1934.

Chapman was a football genius.

He flexed the iron hand in the velvet glove to inject the pride, passion and loyalty into the club that Arsenal have continued to demand from management, players, staff and supporters to this very day. He brought 'Big Football' to the metropolis by building an Arsenal team that equalled and then surpassed the record feats of his beloved Huddersfield Town.

A comparison of the two clubs' performances under Chapman's management over five seasons makes fascinating reading:

Club	Seasons	P	W	D	L	For	Against
Huddersfield	1922–27	210	105	66	39	357	213
Arsenal	1930–35	210	123	49	38	525	261

Chapman's tactics

Chapman groomed some of the finest players in the land and then adopted the 'stopper' centre-half system to achieve the best possible results from the squad he had nurtured.

Centre-backs were given a roving commision in the mid-1920s. It was nothing in those days to see a big central defender storming through midfield to help his attack.

Chapman preferred his centre-half to be anchored to the edge of his penalty area where he could control a zone. This demanded that his inside-forwards should play deep, with two flying wingers ready to break whenever Arsenal gained possession.

Ivan Sharpe, a leading football authority of that period, made this observation of mighty Arsenal's system under Chapman: 'It was David

Jack and Joe Hulme on the right, and Alex James and Cliff Bastin on the other wing. A contrast in style with the same end product – ball in the net.'

Early setbacks

These flashes of magic, which were to enliven Highbury in Chapman's two Championships with Arsenal in 1930–31 and 1932–33 and his F.A. Cup triumph in 1930, were a long way off when he launched his new career with a disastrous 1–0 defeat by the old enemy Spurs on 29 August 1925.

Skippering Arsenal that Saturday – the first day of the revolutionary new off-side law – was Charlie Buchan, Chapman's first signing, whose birthplace was close to Arsenal's old ground in Plumstead.

Buchan had been associated with the 'Gunners' as a youngster but in a row with manager George Morrell over an expenses claim, he had walked out, and eventually launched an outstanding career as a striker with Sunderland.

Chairman Norris had refused to pay Sunderland's asking price of £4000 for the 33-year-old Buchan, but the Roker club were persuaded to part with their star player when Arsenal bid £2000 with the promise of £100 for every goal he scored in his first season.

Sunderland jumped at the offer and Buchan weighed in with 19 League goals and two in the F.A. Cup. The Highbury supporters got used to saying: 'There goes another £100' whenever Buchan danced into the penalty area.

Bill Harper, a goalkeeper, arrived from Hibs for £5000 but Buchan was still carping about money, insisting that Arsenal pay him compensation for the likely loss of revenue on a sports shop he ran in Sunderland.

Norris made an illegal payment to Buchan which later came to light and resulted in the Football League finding the Arsenal Chairman guilty of financial irregularities. He was not allowed to take any further part in football; but the man who did so much for Arsenal, despite being so disliked, lived to see his beloved Gunners win the Cup and the League before his death.

Finding the winning formula

If Buchan was the best known Arsenal player of Chapman's first season, Bob John, a wing-half, was the man whose clever control and prompting from midfield made the team tick. He went on to make 421 First Division appearances, a club record which remained intact until George Armstrong smashed it in his 600 match run.

Chapman revived Jimmy Brain's career by moving him from inside-forward to spearhead, a change of position which resulted in Brain cracking a club record 33 goals in 1925–26.

Joe Hulme, a winger for York and Blackburn and just about the fastest player in the country, brought his wisecracking fun to the dressing room. Despite that early setback against Spurs and a 7–0 thrashing by Newcastle, Chapman's first Arsenal team charged into second place in the table by the end of the 1925–26 season.

Who should beat them to the title to make it a hat-trick of Championships? No lesser club than Huddersfield Town!

Arsenal were to finish 11th, 10th, 9th and 14th over the next four years as Chapman shuffled his playing pack to find a winning formula.

His second season in charge was saved by Arsenal's first appearance in an F.A. Cup Final. They beat Sheffield United, Port Vale, Liverpool, Wolves and Southampton on their way to a Final against Cardiff City.

The Final, broadcast on radio for the first time, was a nightmare for Arsenal's Welsh goalkeeper Dan Lewis. He fluffed a weak shot from Hugh Ferguson with 16 minutes left, and in trying to retrieve the situation, turned the ball into his own net.

In a flash of anger after the game, Lewis was seen to hurl his losers' medal into the mud. Bob John, retrieving the medal, said warmly: 'Don't worry Dan, you'll get another chance.'

Sadly, when Arsenal reached the 1930 Final, Lewis had been replaced by Charlie Preedy.

Drinking to success

Chapman's team-building continued. Charlie Jones, a Welsh international winger, and Herbie Roberts, a tall 21-year-old centre-half, arrived from Nottingham Forest and Oswestry respectively.

A 19-year-old milkman was picked up from non-League Kettering. He went by the name of Eddie Hapgood: a small, stocky, fitness fanatic who was destined for greatness in the Arsenal and England shirts of the 1930s.

Poor Hapgood suffered an unhappy introduction to Highbury. He lost the whole of his £10 signing-on fee to a gang of card-sharks on the train from Kettering to London.

David Jack, tall, stylish and cultured, was offered for transfer by Bolton Wanderers at the end of the 1927–28 season. The invitation sent Chapman and his assistant George Allison hurrying up North. Bolton demanded £13,000 for Jack, and Chapman knocked them down to £11,500; but when the Burnden Park officials arrived at the Euston Hotel in London to settle the arrangements, Chapman decided to leave nothing to chance. Bob Wall, later to become a powerhouse official behind the scenes but then launching his career as secretary-assistant to Chapman, tells this story of Chapman's cloak-and-dagger preparations for the meeting.

'We arrived at the hotel half-an-hour early. Chapman immediately went into the lounge bar. He called a waiter, placed two pound notes in his hand and said: "George, this is Mr Wall, my assistant. He will drink whisky and dry ginger. I will drink gin and tonic. We shall be joined by guests. They will drink whatever they like. See that our guests are given double of everything, but Mr Wall's whisky and ginger will contain no whisky, and my gin and tonic will contain no gin." '

What should have been a difficult meeting between the two sides up North had become an amiable affair by the time the Bolton officials walked out of the hotel on wobbly legs to catch the train home!

Herbert Chapman played his finest card to beat off First Division giants Aston Villa, Liverpool and Manchester City for Alex James.

Transfer-listed by Preston in June 1929, Arsenal netted their prize capture for a mere £8750.

Star treatment
If Chapman had a weakness, it could be said he offered preferential treatment to his star players.

Alex James, one of the Wembley wizards who destroyed England in Scotland's 5–1 victory at Wembley in 1928, was allowed to stay in bed until noon when Arsenal were playing at home.

The former Manchester United manager Sir Matt Busby paid Alex this compliment: 'They talk today about middle men as if they were a modern invention. In the magnificent Arsenal of the early thirties, James was the great creator from the middle . . . The number of goals created from rearguard beginnings by Alex James were the most significant factor in Arsenal's greatness.'

A royal Cup Final
Cliff Bastin was a youngster from Exeter who had played for England Schoolboys. He mixed pace and masterly control of a football with an unerring eye for the target – and he was the final cog Chapman needed to complete the Arsenal machine.

Hulme, Jack, Lambert, James and Bastin would take some beating as an attacking formation, and that was the line-up Arsenal paraded at Wembley in 1930 when they shrugged off a disappointing First Division campaign to take on mighty Huddersfield, Chapman's old club.

The Cup Final on 26 April 1930 was attended by King George V. The Arsenal team comprised

Alex James (on the right) – one of the best-ever British footballers.

Charlie Preedy; Tom Parker, Eddie Hapgood; Alf Baker, Bill Seddon, Bob John; Joe Hulme, David Jack, Jack Lambert, Alex James and Cliff Bastin.

Arsenal stole a shock lead in the 17th minute from a move that had been planned in the team coach on the way to Wembley. James, fouled 40 yards from Huddersfield's goal, set Bastin on his way from a quickly taken free-kick, sprinted for a return pass from the flying winger, and thrashed the ball into Huddersfield's net.

With just seven minutes left James slipped the ball to Lambert on a long run from the half-way line and the striker rewarded his supplier with a stunning goal to win the Cup for the first time in Arsenal's history.

A stadium built for success

Meanwhile, Highbury was being quietly transformed into one of the world's most salubrious stadiums. The Princess of Wales braved a cold, windy day to open a new stand in December 1932. The west stand was built to accommodate more than 20,000 supporters, 4000 seated.

Chapman even had the impudence to invite the London Underground authorities to change the name of the Gillespie road station to 'Arsenal'.

Inspired by their success at Wembley in 1930, Arsenal swept all before them in establishing a record total of 66 points in winning the Championship in 1930–31.

Cup Final Hero Jack Lambert weighed-in with a then-record tally of 38 League goals as the Gunners blasted their way to 28 wins.

The team that season is considered by some to be Arsenal's finest ever. It read: Ted Harper; Tom Parker, Eddie Hapgood, Herbie Roberts; Charlie Jones, Bob John; Joe Hulme, David Jack, Jack Lambert, Alex James, Cliff Bastin.

Much of the credit for Arsenal's success at this time was heaped upon Tom Whittaker, coach, physiotherapist and father-figure to most of the squad.

Bernard Joy, who was to become a commanding figure in later years and a first rate journalist when his football career ended, said of Whittaker: 'Chapman's success would have been impossible without Whittaker.'

Injury time

Arsenal's success in Cup and Championship in the two previous seasons generated the belief at Highbury that they could pull off the League and Cup Double in 1931–32.

Everton clinched the title with Arsenal running them close in second place, but they were not to be denied a place in the 1932 F.A. Cup Final against old rivals Newcastle.

Alex James was ruled out through injury in what would have been a comical mishap if it had not meant so much to his career and to the club.

The wee wizard had been passed fit for the game when Whittaker launched himself into a friendly tackle on Alex for the benefit of a newspaper photographer. To Whittaker's horror, James reeled away in agony, clutching his knee . . . and was ruled out for the big game.

George Male, signed from London amateur club Clapton earlier in the season, was to form one of the greatest full-back pairings in League history when he joined Hapgood as Arsenal's last line of defence.

They both went on to captain England, but the fast, determined and rugged Male appeared at half-back in the 1932 Final.

Arsenal started where they left off in 1930 by scoring through a Bob John header to lead Newcastle 1–0. The Magpies equalised through one of the most controversial goals ever seen in the famous stadium.

Their inside-forward Jimmy Richardson chased a long ball which appeared to cross the goal-line, but as the Arsenal defence relaxed, believing the ball was out of play, Richardson hooked the ball into the centre, and Jack Allen scored.

Allen scored a second goal after the interval to relegate Arsenal to runners-up.

Fire from the Gunners
Denis Hill-Wood, who had succeeded the discredited Norris as Chairman, was now to see his visionary ideals materialise as Arsenal took the First Division by storm over the next three years and walked off with a hat-trick of League Championships.

Hulme and Bastin continued to cut swathes through static defences on their fast, raiding touchline runs, and, as always, James supplied the ammunition for all the Gunners' cannon-fire. Two Championship campaigns, in 1932–33 and 1934–35, ended in Arsenal becoming the only team to score more than 100 League goals.

Sockless soccer

The only blot on the landscape of London N5 in this period of rampant Championship success was the little matter of a crushing Third Round defeat by Third Division Walsall in the 1932–33 F.A. Cup.

It is true that Arsenal were decimated by illness, but they still had seven of their regulars on view at Fellows Park. The Gunners had no answer to Walsall's mighty tackling and Gilbert Alsop and Billy Sheppard, from a penalty, scored the goals that made them famous.

Perhaps an episode in the Gunners' dressing room before the game should have served a warning of what was to follow. Charlie Walsh, plucked from the reserves, was told by Chapman that he expected great things from the lad. 'I'm ready to play the game of my life, sir,' replied Walsh. Quick as a flash, Chapman countered: 'Well, you'd better put your stockings on or the crowd will laugh at you.'

Walsh was so nervous he had put his boots on before his socks!

A Christmas cracker!

Wilf Copping, iron-man of Leeds, and Jack Crayston from Bradford replaced Charlie Jones and Bob John over this period; but it was old hand Jack Lambert who set the standards in the first Championship campaign of 1932–33 when he scored five goals in a 9–2 defeat of Sheffield United on Christmas Eve.

By now Bastin was a manager's dream, a maker and taker of goals, a rare quality in wingers throughout football history. He scored 33 goals

that season, which has remained a Football
League record for a winger.

The vision of Herbert Chapman
The 1933–34 campaign was marred by the death
of Herbert Chapman at the age of 55.

In his time at Arsenal he commanded arguably
the highest salary of any League boss. He earned
£2000 in his first season at Highbury. He was a
tough, uncompromising figure. He once cancelled Joe Hulme's weekend off in Lancashire
because his two-goals on the Saturday had been
insufficient.

He refused permission for any of the Arsenal
staff to go home before they had knocked on his
door and enquired: 'Is there anything more for
me to do, sir?'

Herbert Chapman's vision on arrival at Highbury was to build the greatest football team in the
world. Few could argue that the team he
launched on the 1933–34 campaign were not the
best of all time. What a shame that he did not live
to see them win the Championship.

A bust of Herbert Chapman, sculpted by Jacob
Epstein, stands proudly in the entrance hall of
the East Stand as a permanent memorial.

Following in Chapman's footsteps
Darlington-born George Allison was chosen by
Arsenal to take on the hardest job in football . . .
to follow Herbert Chapman.

He took the job towards the end of the 1933–34
season with curious credentials. His football pedigree was impeccable. A supporter of Arsenal
since their Woolwich days, he had been a director

since the early 1920s. He had also built a formidable reputation as a broadcaster. It was George Allison who delivered the first radio commentary from a football match at the 1927 Cup Final; but now, seven years later, he was moving into an even more demanding role.

With Joe Shaw operating as team manager, John Peters as secretary and Tom Whittaker as trainer, Allison moved from the boardroom to the manager's office to begin a reign that was to see Arsenal win more trophies (three Championships and the F.A. Cup) than under Chapman.

He saw Arsenal to the League title in 1934 and again in 1934–35, and three seasons later they did it again to win in 1937–38.

He lacked Chapman's common touch in dealing with players, but he knew a good player when he saw one. He made Southampton's prolific goal-scorer Ted Drake his first signing in March 1934. Drake rewarded Allison by scorching to a personal haul of 42 League goals in the Championship-winning 1934–35 season: a club record that stands today.

On 14 December 1935 Drake scored six goals against Aston Villa with his first six shots and went on to score a seventh to equal the First Division record set by Jimmy Ross of Preston North End way back in 1888.

But Arsenal's success that season was to come in the F.A. Cup, not the League. They clinched the trophy for the second time in six years when a Ted Drake effort against Sheffield United provided the only goal of the game.

By now the great team Chapman had built was beginning to show cracks. Bastin, Hulme and

James were over the top. But Arsenal astonished even themselves by making all the running in the 1936–37 season before allowing Manchester City to pip them to the post.

Alex James, the greatest of all the Gunners, played his last League game for Arsenal against Bolton on 1 May 1937.

With the great stalwarts of Arsenal's glory years in decline, the Gunners astonished their supporters by winning the Championship for the fifth time in eight years at the end of the 1937–38 season.

A tall lanky centre-half named Bernard Joy had replaced Roberts, and George Hunt had made the short journey from Spurs to partner Drake in attack. The only survivors from the glory days were Bastin and Male.

Pre-war games

Arsenal paraded their expensive new signing Bryn Jones for the start of the 1938–39 season. Allison had shattered the record £11,500 fee Arsenal had paid Bolton for David Jack, with the transfer of the Welshman from Wolves for £14,000.

A gifted provider of chances at Wolves, Jones never settled to the task of treading in the footsteps of the great Alex James.

Arsenal finished a disappointing fifth in the last season before the Second World War.

Many of Arsenal's pre-war stars were to participate in wartime football, but the Gunners would clearly need to find another Herbert Chapman if they were to plug the holes that were beginning to appear in the fabric of their Highbury haven.

Chapter Three

Whittaker's Wonders

A CRUSHING defeat at Wolverhampton at the beginning of the 1946–47 season convinced George Allison his team needed strengthening.

Players, approaching their prime in 1939, were now in rapid decline. The health of others had been damaged by the deprivation and the sheer hell of seeing action on the battle fronts.

Others had simply lost their cutting edge through inactivity and were never to reproduce the dynamic physical effort that had persuaded the Arsenal management to hire them in the first place.

Allison pinned his faith in a couple of old troopers in that first season after the war. He forked out £7000 for 32-year-old Joe Mercer, the bandy-legged genius of Everton's midfield.

The attack was strengthened by the arrival of Ronnie Rooke, three years older than Mercer but still a danger in the penalty area. The former Fulham 'poacher' rewarded Allison's belief in his goal-scoring talents by scoring 21 goals in 24 First Division games, while Reg Lewis, who started the season with an 11-goal burst in 10 games, went on to contribute 29 strikes.

Huge crowds were flooding onto the terraces at Highbury as buses, trams, tubes and trains made Highbury their target on Saturdays. Arsenal captured the mood of the nation: 'The bad times are over, let's have a ball.'

New management

After four decades of total commitment to the Arsenal cause, George Allison decided the demands of post-war management were too great and retired for a 'less strenuous life' at the end of the season.

Arsenal looked no further than Tom Whittaker to find a replacement for Allison in the summer of 1947. The sensitive hands that had worked wonders on strains, pulls, bruises and dislocations were now to be employed pulling strings at one of the world's foremost clubs.

Joe Shaw returned from Chelsea to assist Whittaker, who wasted no time signing Archie Macaulay from Brentford on the strength of rave reports about the Scottish international winghalf, and Don Roper was persuaded to leave his beloved Southampton.

A 3–1 victory over Sunderland at Highbury gave Whittaker the perfect start to what was to become a remarkable first season in management.

When Leslie Compton, the elder of Arsenal's two famous cricketing brothers, returned from summer service with Middlesex, the Gunners had won six games on the trot.

Whittaker handed his Club Captain Compton the ball for the game at Preston, but just when the team was leaving the dressing room at Deepdale, Compton made a moving gesture.

'If you don't mind Mr Whittaker, I think Joe should have this' said Compton, handing the ball to Mercer, who had led the side in the opening games.

Joe Mercer led the team on to the pitch, and retained the captaincy for a season that was to see him raise the Championship trophy for the first time by an Arsenal captain since 1938.

By now Denis Compton was in the team after an operation on a knee that was to give him trouble for most of his football and cricket careers. His promotion to the team for the match against Burnley drew a massive gate. Who could fail to be fired by his brilliance in scoring 17 centuries and more than 3000 runs in the 1947 cricket season?

Strengthening the team

Whittaker was shrewd in the transfer market but cautious in his choice (he watched Don Roper play for Southampton at least 10 times before offering him a contract). He had taken care to strengthen that 1948 title-winning team when the existing squad was giving most clubs in the First Division a good hiding.

Cliff Holton, a forward with a thunderbolt shot, was secured from Oxford City in November 1947; Peter Goring came from Cheltenham Town in Janary 1948; and Alex Forbes was good enough in Sheffield United's midfield to persuade Whittaker to spend £12,000.

It took the dynamic Forbes just eight minutes to repay some of that transfer outlay. His dance back to the centre circle after scoring the equaliser against Wolves confirmed his overwhelming commitment to Arsenal – he had turned down an opportunity to play professional ice hockey.

Doug Lishman, a proven goal-scorer in the Third Division, was bought from Walsall in May 1948, and Arsenal had a dynamic start to the season in the showpiece Charity Shield game against Cup-holders Manchester United. They led 3–0 in just five minutes through Bryn Jones, Reg Lewis and Ronnie Rooke. However, that success was not to be maintained in the League campaign. They never truly got into their stride, finishing fifth in the table behind Champions Portsmouth.

A further blow to the team came with the departure of Ronnie Rooke, who left Highbury to become player-manager at Crystal Palace at the age of 37. He made only 88 First Division appearances, but what an impact he had! He tormented plenty of defences in his scoring of 68 goals.

The 1950 Cup Final

Arsenal shrugged off another disappointing League season to scorch a red trail to Wembley. Reg Lewis set them on their way by scoring the only goal of a cliff-hanging Third Round tie against Sheffield Wednesday, unbeaten in three months, with only 13 seconds of the game remaining.

It took Arsenal's Welshman Walley Barnes to sink all-Welsh Swansea in the Fourth Round. The Second Division visitors to Highbury put up a magnificent fight till Barnes settled the match with a penalty.

Reg Lewis and Denis Compton destroyed Burnley in the Fifth Round, and Reg Lewis disposed of Arsenal's Sixth Round opponents Leeds

38

United to put them in the semi-finals.

Incredibly, Arsenal had been drawn at home in all five Cup-ties, and they only had a mile or two to travel for their semi-final game against Chelsea, played at White Hart Lane.

Roy Bentley, fast emerging as one of the best young centre-forwards in the country, sent Chelsea racing into a 2–0 lead, which, on Arsenal's form in the League and earlier Cup-ties, looked an unassailable advantage.

A mistake by Chelsea's goalkeeper Harry Medhurst just before half time was to give Arsenal an opportunity to seize some of the initiative Chelsea had cornered.

Freddie Cox, one of those players whose best years had been sacrificed in the war, propelled a corner with the outside of his boot into Chelsea's goal-mouth. Before goalkeeper Medhurst could move, the ball was nestling in the net.

Leslie Compton totally ignored Joe Mercer's plea for him to remain in defence when he charged upfield to head brother Denis's corner into Chelsea's goal for the equaliser 15 minutes from the end.

Before the replay the following Wednesday, Freddie Cox's wife, Eileen, had admitted to a vivid dream in which her husband had scored the goal that shot Arsenal into the Cup Final.

The unbelievable happened! The score was Arsenal 1, Chelsea 0. The scorer was Freddie Cox, in extra-time.

The newspapers saw Mercer as a folk-hero and their headlines gave the 1950 Cup Final a romantically compelling appeal. Could the veteran Joe Mercer crown an outstanding career by winning the Cup against Liverpool?

The Football Writers' Association was hardly impartial in its judgement on the eve of the big game when Joe Mercer stepped up to receive the coveted Footballer of the Year award.

Jimmy Logie, the smallest player in the Arsenal team, played the game of his life in midfield. Logie, spotting Liverpool's defence lying square, punctured it after only 17 minutes to send Reg Lewis racing through the hole to put the Gunners one up.

Seventeen minutes into the second half, Freddie Cox saw another opening to set up Lewis for a second goal and hand Joe Mercer the winner's medal to climax his extraordinary career.

Denis Compton's decision to make Wembley his farewell appearance for Arsenal had been exploited cleverly by Tom Whittaker in his talk at half-time.

The cricketer-footballer, failing to make any impact in the first half, was taken aside by Whittaker and given some stern advice: 'You've got 45 minutes left of your soccer career. I want you to go out there and give it every ounce you possibly can, Denis,' said Whittaker. Compton produced the form after the break that had rendered him one of the great all-round sportsmen of his age.

Leslie Compton, now 38, thought nothing of retirement. Indeed, on 15 November 1950 he became the oldest player to make his début for England with his part in a 4–2 win over Wales.

Losing their way

Arsenal's hopes of winning the Championship in the 1950–51 season probably collapsed when their leading scorer Doug Lishman broke his leg on Christmas Day.

The Gunners were leading the pack when first Lishman and then George Swindin were badly injured against Stoke City. Lishman, in particular, was missed because of his goal-scoring that season. He had bagged 16 by the time he was stretchered off, four of them coming against Sunderland, and by the time he was fit to return, Arsenal had lost their way to finish fifth.

By the start of the 1951–52 season the immaculate Ray Daniel had succeeded Leslie Compton at centre-half, George Swindin had recovered from injury, Walley Barnes had become one of the best full-backs in the First Division, and Mercer, Roper, Logie and Forbes were making decisive contributions.

The attack was led by Lishman and Holton, whose reputation for scoring goals from outside the penalty area made him a schoolboy favourite.

By the end of the season Arsenal were just three games from pulling off the League and Cup Double. They finished up with nothing.

Arsenal's assault on Wembley involved a repeat of the F.A. Cup semi-final game against Chelsea. Again it went to a replay at White Hart Lane, and again that great Cup-fighter Freddie Cox stole the show with a two-goal display.

Arsenal's build-up to Wembley resembled a mad comedy. Jimmy Logie climbed out of a hospital bed to play in the Final and Ray Daniel appeared from the tunnel with a plaster-cast pro-

41

tecting the arm he had broken at Blackpool.

Inspired by Doug Lishman, Arsenal started the 1952 Final against Newcastle United in the all-attacking fashion they had produced in the second-half against Liverpool two years earlier.

Lishman went close with a fierce drive in the early stages; but when Arsenal were beginning to dominate the game, Walley Barnes twisted his knee just before half-time and became a passenger for the rest of the game.

Memorable seasons

The 1952–53 season was memorable for at least two reasons. Whittaker's wonders won the Championship for a record seventh time, and Jimmy Logie, so often overlooked by selectors, was given his first Scotland cap at the age of 33.

Jack Kelsey had emerged as a worthy successor to George Swindin. He was to make 54 appearances in goal for Wales between 1954–62, but in his début season for Arsenal he was showing the first glimpses of the natural talent that would give him a place alongside some of the great British goalkeepers since the war.

The final League table read: Arsenal 54 points, Preston 54 points. Arsenal got the verdict on goal average!

Mercer was not to say goodbye for another year, but a player of equal renown was to make his début for Arsenal on 19 September 1953. Tommy Lawton, recognised as the finest spearhead in the country when he led the Everton attack before the War, was signed from Brentwood where he was struggling as player-manager.

**Tom Whittaker, who steered Arsenal to two
Championships and the F.A. Cup.**

Tom Whittaker defended his decision to sign the 34-year-old Lawton by recalling Ronnie Rooke's massive contribution as a so-called ageing striker.

But the spark of the 1952–53 season was missing in 1953–54 and 1954–55. Arsenal slumped to mid-table.

The Lawton deal never succeeded; Jimmy Logie slipped quietly into life at non-League Gravesend; and Joe Mercer left centre stage as he had begun his Arsenal career – in dramatic fashion. He broke his leg in a collision with team-mate Joe Wade on 10 April 1954. With a cheery wave from his stretcher, he left hardly a dry eye at Highbury as he disappeared into history.

The 1955–56 season – Arsenal came fifth behind Manchester United – saw the departure of Doug Lishman to Nottingham Forest with a record of which he was proud. He averaged a goal every two games, scoring 125 goals in 226 League matches for the Gunners.

In October 1956, Arsenal lost their manager Tom Whittaker. He died in University College Hospital on Wednesday, 24 October, 1956.

He had been in poor health for some time and had never fully recovered from an operation earlier that year. Like the legendary Herbert Chapman, he died as he would have wished – in the hot seat.

No bronze bust of Tom Whittaker would appear in Arsenal's marble halls; but no manager since Herbert Chapman had done more to restore the Gunners to the heights they had scaled between the two great wars.

Chapter Four

Trouble – then Double

The next few years were to see once-mighty Arsenal limp through one of the bleakest periods in the club's long and proud history.

Little of the bubbly optimism inspired by the launch of the Beatles and the Rolling Stones in the 'Swinging Sixties' was reflected in the Gunners' performances. Managers arrived and departed, players came and went, and the hardcore of Arsenal supporters were forced to suffer in silence on Highbury's North Bank.

Arsenal's only claim to anything approaching the heady success of their glory days were two successive appearances in the League Cup Final in 1968 and 1969 – which ended in defeat on both occasions.

A Terry Cooper goal for Leeds United divided the sides in the Wembley Final of 1968. Worse was to follow in 1969 when Third Division Swindon performed one of the most swashbuckling acts in Wembley history, upsetting Arsenal's hopes for a second time.

Crayston's reign
Jack Crayston, a big wing-half who had propelled throw-ins over freak distances in two League

Championship campaigns and the 1936 F.A. Cup Final, was the man in charge at the start of this period of decline.

Known as 'Gentleman Jack' – a 13-stone gentleman who had fought awesomely on the pitch for England and Arsenal – Crayston replaced the late Tom Whittaker in December 1956.

A Welshman and a Scot gave Crayston good cause for optimism in his first season. Derek Tapscott cracked 25 League goals and David Herd, son of former Scottish international Alec, was blossoming into one of the most exciting strikers in the game.

They helped Arsenal finish fifth in the League, 14 points adrift of 1956–57 Champions Manchester United.

Yet Crayston inherited player problems from the moment he took office. Vic Groves, a £20,000 recruit, had slapped in a transfer request after failing to establish himself in more than a year at the club.

However, Crayston's sympathetic understanding of the restless star's problems led to a change of attitude from Groves, who got married, moved into a new house, and began to offer Arsenal the service on the pitch that had encouraged the club to buy him in the first place.

Arsenal showed poor League form in 1957–58 – they finished 12th in the First Division only eight points above bottom club Sheffield Wednesday. The club plunged into crisis, and Crayston resigned.

Swindin's years

George Swindin, the former Arsenal goalkeeper, was given the job of reviving the club's fortunes. He was to last four years. One of his first acts in the hot-seat was to persuade a tough, wise-cracking Scott named Tommy Docherty to leave Preston North End for Arsenal.

Persuade? The 'Doc' leapt at the chance, forgetting even to discuss terms in his eagerness to pull on the famous red shirt. Docherty rewarded Swindin by scoring a goal on his League début against Burnley at Highbury.

The dynamic Cliff Holton was allowed to take his thunderous shooting to Watford. Derek Tapscott drifted off back to Wales proud of his 60 odd goals in 119 First Division games. Meanwhile Swindin ducked and dived in an effort to find a winning formula.

Jackie Henderson, a big, raw-boned Scot, announced his arrival from Wolves with a two-goal burst to sink West Bromich Albion; Billy McCullough, an all-action full-back, arrived from Portadown; Jim Standen, recruited by Crayston, was given his chance in goal when Welsh giant Jack Kelsey was injured; and Danny Clapton, Arsenal's quicksilver winger, won his first and only England cap as Arsenal began to show the form in 1958–59 that their new manager was demanding.

Arsenal finished third in the table behind Wolves and Manchester United, but 20 players had left Highbury in Swindin's blitz on a second-rate squad not worthy of Arsenal. Sadly, all the good work had little effect. The club finished 13th in 1959–60.

47

Not all Swindin's transfer dealings were successful. Mel Charles, brother of Wales, Leeds and Juventus giant John, needed two knee operations in a short and unsuccessful time at Highbury before he went to Cardiff; and Cliff Jones, another star Welshman, preferred to join Bill Nicholson's Spurs rather than Arsenal.

A legal battle

Swindin was not a man to allow disappointments to curb his ambitions for Arsenal. He signed George Eastham, the brilliant, ball-playing inside-forward at Newcastle United for £47,000 in November 1960.

At first, the Newcastle directors blocked the move. In those days a player was tied to a club for life if the club wanted to keep him. Eastham demanded the right to move, and after joining Arsenal fought a legal battle in the courts which was to have ramifications for all professional footballers.

Eastham v Newcastle United in the High Court in 1963 was to see the footballer win his case. The Football League had to instruct all member clubs to draw up contracts for players. The Arsenal fans were far more interested in Eastham's ability to make a football 'talk'. He won 19 England caps in his six year career at Highbury.

Disappointments and appointments

The 1960–61 and 1961–62 seasons were major disappointments for Swindin, who, from his office in Highbury, could almost hear the 'Glory, Glory' adulation that was being heaped upon Tottenham's Double-winning side.

Above: **Arsenal players with the F.A. Cup after victory against Huddersfield, 1930. L to R: Hulme, Seddon, Parker, Preedy, Bastin.**

Below: **Alex James practising at Highbury, August 1933.**

Left: **Bastin taking a shot at goal in the F.A. Cup Final, 1936, when Arsenal defeated Sheffield United 1–0.**

Right: **1950 F.A. Cup Winners after defeating Liverpool 2–0. Back, L to R: Whittaker (manager), Compton, Scott, Swindon, Barnes, Milne (trainer). Front, L to R: Forbes, Cox, Logie, Mercer, Goring, Lewis, Compton.**

BBC Hulton Picture Library

BBC Hulton Picture Library

Above: **February 1939. Chelsea's goalkeeper dives to save after Drake (with fist in the air) has headed the ball towards the goal.**

Right: **The civic welcome after Arsenal won the 'Double' in 1971.**

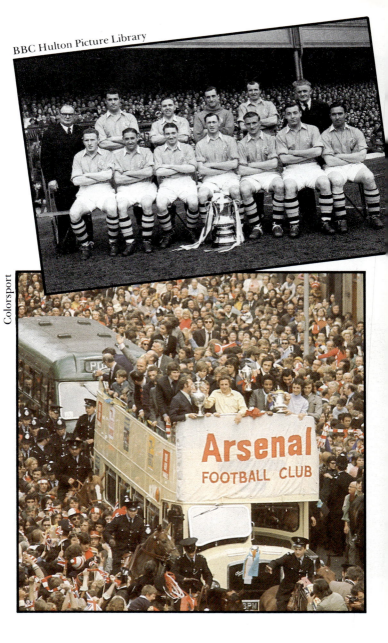

Arsenal
FOOTBALL CLUB

Left: **Pat Jennings in action.**

Allsport

Colorsport

Above: **Charlie George (arm in the air) celebrates a goal against Chelsea.**

Left: **Charlie Nicholas (behind Liverpool's goalkeeper Bruce Grobbelaar) scores Arsenal's first goal in the 1987 Littlewoods Cup Final.**

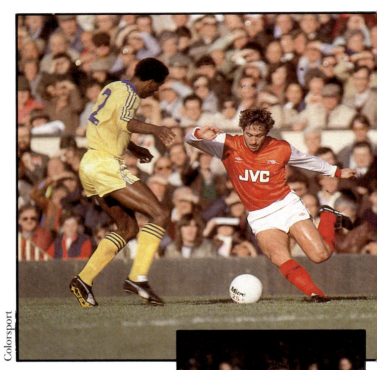

Above: **Kenny Sansom in action against Nottingham Forest.**

Right: **Liam Brady at full pace.**

Above: **Tony Adams beats his West Ham opponent to the ball.**

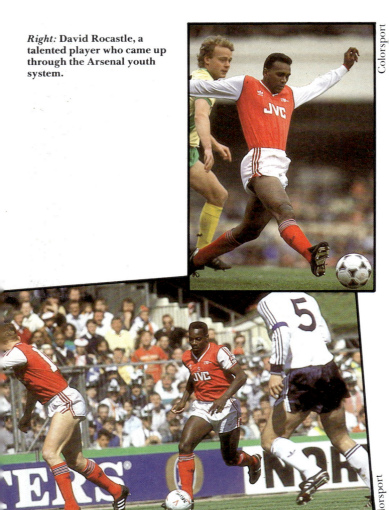

Right: David Rocastle, a talented player who came up through the Arsenal youth system.

Colorsport

Colorsport

Above: Michael Thomas (centre) playing against Luton in the 1988 Littlewoods Cup Final.

Bertie Mee, later to become one of Arsenal's finest managers, arrived almost unannounced to take charge of the physio treatment room.

The arrival of Eddie Clamp, iron-man in the Wolves defence, did nothing to stop the rot and George Swindin, bitterly disappointed at his failure to revive the club he had served so well as a goalkeeper, resigned before the start of the 1962–63 season.

Since the appointment of the nationally celebrated Herbert Chapman, the Arsenal board had resisted the temptation to go for a big name, preferring to appoint a manager from within the ranks.

They changed their policy with the arrival of Billy Wright, the great Wolves servant who had won a record 105 England caps and was the Football Association's 'golden boy' after captaining his country on 90 occasions.

Billy Wright arrives

Wright's appointment received massive coverage in the sports pages of national newspapers. His marriage to top singing star Joy Beverley, of Beverley Sisters fame, earned the new Arsenal manager almost as much publicity on the front pages as it did on the back sports pages.

He staked his reputation on £70,000 Torino striker Joe Baker, who had made his name for Hibernian in the Scottish League.

Terry Neill, a strong Northern Ireland defender, was given the captaincy, with Geoff Strong and John Barnwell lining up at inside-forward alongside the newly recruited Baker.

Wright launched his Highbury career with a victory over Orient, but that 1962–63 season was to see no rapid improvement in the club's League form. The most encouraging aspect of that season was the form of Baker and Strong, who scored more than 50 goals between them.

Only Champions Liverpool scored more goals than Arsenal in 1963–64 when the Baker-Strong spearhead pulverised defences. They both scored more than 30 League and Cup goals apiece, but only bottom clubs Ipswich and Birmingham let in more goals in the First Division.

Arsenal enjoyed their first taste of European competition that season in the Inter-Cities Fairs Cup. Part-timers Staevnet, of Denmark, were overwhelmed by Baker and Strong hat-tricks, but Standard Liège cancelled out a McCullough goal to win handsomely.

Exit another manager

The 1964–65 campaign saw England right-back Don Howe in the Arsenal line-up. A tall, commanding defender for West Bromwich Albion, he brought strength to the Gunner's defence.

Yet Wright's judgement was in question after Howe's nightmare début when Liverpool's Peter Thompson roasted him down the touchline at Anfield. The match was screened that night in the BBC's *Match of the Day* – the first time the programme was networked.

Geoff Strong's general form and his appearance in that match prompted the Liverpool manager Bill Shankly to make a bid for the Arsenal striker, which resulted in Strong's move to Anfield in November 1964.

Scottish international Frank McLintock was picked up from Leicester City. He had risen to prominence as a cultured wing-half in the midland club's two F.A. Cup Final appearances in the early sixties.

Third Division Peterborough United turned 'David' to slay 'Goliath' Arsenal in a tragic F.A. Cup exit. Their place of 13th in the First Division brought cries for a big shake-up to the ears of the beleaguered Billy Wright.

The Arsenal board's decision to sack one of England's favourite sons shook him to the core when he returned from holiday with his family to hear the sad news from Chairman Denis Hill-Wood after the 1965–66 season.

How ironic that Billy Wright, a true lion of English football with an outstanding playing career, should see the curtain fall on his football days only a few months before England were to wipe the floor with the rest of the world!

Bertie who?
If Billy Wright was second only to Stan Matthews and Tom Finney as a household name when he arrived at Arsenal, few outside Highbury's marble halls knew much about Bertie Mee when he was named manager before the start of the 1966–67 season.

He was setting no precedent in accepting the job, for physio Tom Whittaker had taken the same route towards the ultimate job, the chance to manage one of the world's most famous clubs.

Bertie Mee cleverly boosted his management team by appointing Dave Sexton as coach. Between them they presented a formidable line-up, equal to the Shankly-Paisley pairing in Liverpool, the Mercer-Allison combination at Manchester City, and the long established double-act of Nicholson and Baily at White Hart Lane.

Mee never shirked a difficult decision, showing his combative style almost as soon as he arrived by off-loading George Eastham to Stoke. He started with a win, at Sunderland; saw his team conquer a West Ham team containing England's three World Cup heroes, Moore, Hurst and Peters; and enjoyed a five game unbeaten sequence before deadly North London rivals Spurs intervened to spoil the party.

The standards had been set and Arsenal were to reward their fans by coming seventh in the League in 1966–67.

Regaining form

Mee's second season in charge saw the arrival of £90,000 striker Bobby Gould. Mee had already exchanged Tommy Baldwin for Chelsea's George Graham, and Bob McNab, a full-back, had been transferred from Huddersfield for £50,000.

Dave Sexton's ambition to manage a club saw his departure for Chelsea with Don Howe (now fully recovered from a broken leg which had virtually ended his career) in harness as chief coach.

League form was to remain as erratic as ever, but Arsenal's progress in the League Cup, the Cinderella of the major competitions in those days, was beginning to gain attention, when they reached Wembley for the first time since 1952.

As Wembley finals go, the Leeds-Arsenal encounter in 1968 was not a classic. One goal, scored by Leeds' Terry Cooper, settled the issue in a dour battle fought out mainly between the two penalty areas.

A much more respectable fourth place in the final table of the 1968–69 season confirmed that, in Mee, Arsenal had found the right manager at last.

Jimmy Robertson, a powerful, free running winger at Spurs, arrived at Highbury to strengthen a squad that was looking strong.

Former schoolteacher Bob Wilson won a regular place in goal. Peter Storey, ruthlessly efficient in the tackle, gave Arsenal ball-winning qualities and the Frank McLintock, Ian Ure, Peter Simpson half-back line had few peers in the First Division.

Arsenal took the League Cup by storm again. Sunderland, Scunthorpe, Liverpool and Blackpool were destroyed by the Gunners, who lined up against Spurs in the two-legged semi-finals.

John Radford used the two games to demonstrate his growing potency in the penalty box and unerring eye for the target. He scored a late winner at Highbury. Just when a Jimmy Greaves goal was keeping the White Hart Lane faithful happy in the return, Radford popped up again to launch the Gunners on course for Wembley for the second year running.

Optimism – and defeat
News that Arsenal would play Third Division Swindon Town at Wembley was greeted with undisguised optimism by Mee's team.

53

No player looked forward to the game with more anticipation than Frank McLintock, yet to gain a winners' medal in three run-outs at Wembley.

But it was Swindon who struck first, through Smart, 34 minutes into the match after Arsenal had piled on early pressure. Could the impossible happen? Wembley seemed poised to stage its biggest upset for years when Bobby Gould equalised with just four minutes of the game left.

With the Gunners' greater fitness they were expected to overpower lowly Swindon in extra-time. But the opposite happened. McLintock was suffering cramp in both legs, McNab was clearly struggling, and Swindon's Don Rogers began to impose his qualities on the famous arena. He stabbed Swindon into the lead from a corner in the first period, but reserved a champagne-popping winner for the final stages when he ran half the length of the pitch to beat Wilson's desperate lunge to make it 3–1. Frank McLintock was now a four times Wembley loser.

Rising stars

Meanwhile, a youngster named Charlie George was rising from school playground football in local Islington. He got the chance to play for Arsenal in the 1969–70 season when Bobby Gould, in tears after scoring the Gunners' only goal at Wembley, was dismissed to the reserves.

Ian Ure was sold to Manchester United to end his six year career, and young Ray Kennedy was drafted into the team to play up front alongside John Radford.

All of these comings and goings were over-shadowed by the glitzy arrival of Peter Marinello for £100,000 from Scottish League Hibernian. Billed as the 'second George Best', the young Scot received film-star treatment from Fleet Street.

He modelled clothes, boosted his bank balance by promoting products, was photographed with pretty girls, and wrote a column for a national newspaper. But could he play?

Marinello was 19 when he arrived in London. His form in the Scottish League as a clever ball-playing forward had encouraged Arsenal to transfer Robertson to Spurs, but the nagging doubt about Marinello's ability to establish himself at Highbury was to haunt him – and Bertie Mee – throughout the duration of his Arsenal career.

European comptition
Meanwhile, Arsenal were beginning to make an impact in European competition for the first time. Dinamo Bacau were crushed in the quarter-finals of the Fairs Cup and not even the presence of Johan Cruyff, Rudi Krol and Wim Suurbier could save Ajax in the semi-finals. Charlie George, with a long range drive and a penalty, and Jon Sammels steered Arsenal to a meeting with Anderlecht.

Ray Kennedy, deputising for the tired Charlie George, gave Arsenal cause for optimism when he scored a late goal in Brussels on 22 April, 1970. He reduced the Anderlecht advantage to 3–1 in the first-leg.

Not even the most diehard Gunner could see much hope of Arsenal overcoming that disadvantage in the second leg at Highbury on 28 April 1970. Fifty-one thousand supporters, most of them wearing red, saw Eddie Kelly offer the Gunners a lifeline with a snap shot after only a few minutes.

Radford headed a second goal, and Sammels sent the North Bank into raptures of song with a killing third goal which sent fans spilling on to the Highbury pitch to embrace their heroes.

Charlie George, the fans' favourite, had his shirt stripped from his body, and Frank McLintock had won a trophy at long last!

Bertie Mee was left to reflect on the fact that he had masterminded Arsenal's first victory campaign in 17 barren seasons.

A breakthrough
Don Howe's words that victory night carried an ominous warning to Arsenal's rivals. 'This can be the big breakthrough.'

The season of 1970–71 was to underline the wisdom of those prophetic words.

But the Radford-Kennedy act was beginning to grow strong. Ray Kennedy cracked a hat-trick in a 4–0 drubbing of Nottingham Forest. By the end of the campaign he was the First Division's fourth highest scorer with 19 goals.

Radford, hat-trick hero of Arsenal's 4–0 home win against Manchester United, was hardly less effective. He cracked 15 goals in the League as Arsenal stormed to their first Championship title since 1953, ahead of Leeds United and Tottenham Hotspur.

The Gunners clinched a record eighth Championship at Spurs with a headed goal by Ray Kennedy. He scored in the dying seconds of a game watched by 51,000 – and with thousands more locked out.

Semi-finals

Arsenal's dream of emulating Tottenham's Double-winning feat of 1960–61 gathered momentum. Arsenal reached the semi-finals of the 1971 F.A Cup.

With Everton and Liverpool called upon to sort out the other semi-final, Arsenal drew unfancied Stoke at Hillsborough. At half-time their Double hopes seemed dead, if not entirely buried. They trailed 2–0. One bizarre goal had seen Peter Storey's attempted clearance fly off Denis Smith's head into Arsenal's net.

Peter Storey, more of a team man than an individualist, made up for his earlier confusion in defence by sending a 20 yard drive past a startled Gordon Banks to make it 2–1.

Arsenal's efforts to equalise were frantic; but with referee Pat Partridge beginning to look at his watch, Mahoney handled McLintock's goalbound header to concede a penalty.

Rarely has a Gunner faced more pressure than penalty expert Storey when he put the ball on the spot just 12 yards from the greatest goalkeeper in the world, Gordon Banks.

Banks shaped to go right, Storey shot to his left, and Arsenal had forced the most unlikely replay.

North and South

Four days later Arsenal put Stoke in their place, beating them 2–0 with goals by Ray Kennedy and

George Graham. Thus a North versus South F.A. Cup Final meeting with mighty Liverpool was set up.

Arsenal squandered several clear-cut chances to win the Cup before the game moved into extra time with the teams deadlocked at 0–0.

Eddie Kelly had replaced the tiring Peter Storey on the hour and Peter Thompson was subbing for Alun Evans in the Liverpool attack. Both substitutes were to have a significant bearing on the result. Thompson sent Steve Heighway free of Pat Rice to beat Bob Wilson on his near post. An instinctive save by Wilson from Brian Hall kept Arsenal in the game, and within 10 minutes of Liverpool's goal, Eddie Kelly had equalised.

Just nine minutes of extra-time remained when Charlie George, exhausted and unable to make his penetrating runs, drove an unstoppable shot beyond the reach of Ray Clemence.

The 20-year-old Highbury hero, who had stood as a schoolboy on the North Bank cheering his favourite Gunners, had waved the wand that conjured the magic League and Cup Double.

Bertie Mee was happy but not fully contented that Wembley day. Many of his ambitions were fulfilled – but Cologne had sent them spinning out of the European Fairs Cup quarter-finals.

'I wouldn't mind the European Cup next season. I know we have done the Double but at the moment it's too much to take in,' said the man who had done more than anyone to restore some pride to the long-suffering club.

Chapter Five

Charlie's their Darling

Arsenal spluttered into gear at the beginning of the 1971–72 season. Don Howe, track-suited mastermind behind their Double-winning performance the previous season, was now trying his hand in management at West Bromwich Albion. His departure could have had a bearing on the Gunners' erratic form in the early weeks.

Bertie Mee saw the chinks appearing in Arsenal's hitherto infallible armour. Never slow to plunge into the transfer market to maintain standards, he cracked the Football League record transfer fee by splashing out £220,000 on Alan Ball.

Few players in the First Division had a pedigree more worthy of mighty Arsenal's reputation than Ball, hero of England's World Cup victory six years before, and a vital component in Everton's Championship winning team of 1970.

Ball's effervescent personality drove a new spirit into the Arsenal's midfield; but despite stringing together a 14 match unbeaten run after their faltering start, the Gunners were unable to catch Champions Derby County. They finished fifth.

The F.A. Cup was a different matter. Swindon, Reading, Derby, Orient, and Stoke (after a replay) all perished as Arsenal launched themselves on Wembley for the second year running.

Leeds United, Arsenal's opponents, were fancied to win the trophy in the Centenary Year of the most thrilling spectacle in English sport.

Arsenal's attack, led by John Radford and Charlie George, backfired as it had done in the League. Allan Clarke scored the only goal of a dull match to hand Leeds the trophy.

Trouble and strife

Not even entry to the quarter-finals of the European Cup could satisfy Bertie Mee as he watched his team go out of the competition to a fine Ajax side led by Cruyff.

Dressing room unrest had not helped Arsenal's cause. One of the rebels, Charlie George (the other was Eddie Kelly), was put on the transfer list and club captain Frank McLintock, the cornerstone of three great seasons, was considered to be too old.

Arsenal bought Coventry's Jeff Blockley for only £20,000 less than they paid Everton for Ball, but that deal was never to harvest the same rewards for the club.

Nevertheless, Arsenal had too many good players to become a team of strugglers overnight. With John Radford and Ray Kennedy back to their best, Arsenal went 15 League games unbeaten and ended the 1972–73 season only three points behind Champions Liverpool.

They reached the F.A. Cup semi-finals with high hopes of making Wembley when Charlie

George's goal was cancelled out by two from Second Division Sunderland.

Difficult days

Arsenal were not to win another trophy until 1979. Crowds became disillusioned. The North Bank's hero Charlie George went to Derby; Frank McLintock and George Graham departed; and Ray Kennedy became Bill Shankly's last purchase when he went to Liverpool for £200,000.

Mee plunged £100,000 on Manchester United's striker Brian Kidd, but he stayed only two years.

The transfer of Alex Cropley from Hibernian to Highbury for £150,000 sums up all that was frustrating about this period for Bertie Mee. Cropley had played fewer than 10 games in Arsenal's midfield when he broke his leg, the injury wrecking what promised to be a glittering career for the Scottish international. He stayed just under two years in an Arsenal career that lasted only 34 games. Charlie George's unhappiness was ended when Dave Mackay persuaded him to join Derby for £90,000. George's problematic last year at Highbury symbolised the growth of player-power in the seventies. Players could wreck dressing-room spirit with one biting remark — and many of them also wrecked their own golden careers through carelessness. It was a gloomy period for English football.

Arsenal's struggle in the mid-seventies was reflected in Alan Ball's disenchantment with Highbury. He lost his captaincy after asking for a transfer; Eddie Kelly was sold to Leicester; and Peter Storey got so fed up he walked out for a couple of weeks and was suspended by the club.

Mee goes – Neill arrives

Not even the promise of a slip of an Irish lad named Liam Brady could influence Bertie Mee to stay in charge of a club that was clearly falling apart. The team he had worked so cleverly to build was in sharp decline, and the man who had been Arsenal's salvation at the start of the seventies announced his retirement at the end of the 1975–76 season.

Mee turned down offers of a directorship at Arsenal to spend a period in the football wilderness; before re-discovering his appetite for the game in a long and fruitful association with Watford as Graham Taylor's assistant.

The Highbury board turned to Terry Neill. Neill was firmly embedded in management at Spurs, but he was prepared to return to the club he had served as a player for more than 10 years.

Alan Ball was transferred to Southampton where he launched the third phase of his outstanding playing career. Terry Neill needed a big name to hoist Arsenal back into the big-time. Arsenal and Spurs embarked on a neck and neck race to sign Malcolm Macdonald from Newcastle.

Supermac

Thunder-boots Macdonald, nicknamed 'Supermac' on Tyneside, chose Arsenal in a transfer deal worth £333,333. He flew by plane to join his new club, boasting he would score 30 goals in his first season. 'Supermouth' got it wrong. He was one out! He cracked 29 fabulous goals that brought Gunners' fans pouring back on to High-

**Liam Brady, a member of Arsenal's highly
successful team of the 1970s.**

bury's once-deserted terraces.

With John Radford's superb career drawing to a close, Macdonald and a bright young striker from the reserves, Frank Stapleton, formed a partnership that was to become one of the First Division's most lethal pairings.

By the end of Macdonald's first season of 1976–77, he and Aston Villa's Scottish striker Andy Gray were top of the First Division tree with 25 League goals apiece.

Disgrace!

Liverpool's domination of the Championship, with Nottingham Forest making a brief intervention to win the title in 1977–78, kept Arsenal down in the League at this period.

An end-of-season tour in the summer of 1977, unpopular with the players, became a nightmare for Neill. Alan Hudson, who had made his name with Chelsea as the Rolls-Royce of their midfield, and the other new-boy Macdonald were sent home in disgrace for drinking and other escapades.

Both were transfer-listed, Macdonald made it up with Neill, but Hudson was never to live up to his former reputation, leaving eventually for Seattle Sounders.

Neill made two acquisitions that summer who were to have a huge influence on the club over the next few years. Don Howe returned to understudy Neill; and Pat Jennings, challenging Ray Clemence and Peter Shilton for the 'golden goal-keeper' award of that era, moved from Spurs to Highbury for £40,000.

Alan Sunderland, Wolves' promising young sharp-shooter, joined Arsenal for £70,000 and England Youth midfielder David Price was drafted into the team.

The blend was almost perfect as Arsenal rode high in the title race. The club reached the League Cup semi-final and made it to Wembley for the F.A. Cup Final.

League Cup – and F.A. Cup defeat

The League Cup captured imaginations. First Hull, then Southampton, and finally Manchester City were swept aside as the Gunners stormed into the semi-finals. They met Liverpool at their best, with old-boy Ray Kennedy wicked enough to give the Reds a one-goal advantage for the return leg at Highbury.

Arsenal's hopes of damaging Liverpool's reputation at home foundered on the brilliance of Ray Clemence's goalkeeping as he produced a series of thrilling saves to deny Frank Stapleton.

But, inspired by Liam Brady's maturing skills in midfield, Arsenal surged into the 1978 F.A. Cup Final for a meeting with Bobby Robson's Ipswich Town.

The little Suffolk club with big ideas hammered Arsenal to defeat, Osborne scoring the only goal.

The Gunners made no excuses for their poor display, but it was common knowledge that Liam Brady and Malcolm Macdonald were carrying injuries. 'We shall return,' vowed a dispirited Terry Neill.

UEFA Cup

Arsenal did return – in 1979, but not before they caused a ripple of excitement in the UEFA Cup by beating Lokomotiv Leipzig and Hajduk Split. The Split game was full of drama. Brady gave Arsenal high hopes of victory with a crucial 'away' goal in a 2–1 defeat in Yugoslavia, but the hero was to turn villain in the second–leg when he was sent off for retaliation under extreme provocation from Split's man-to-man markers. Two Yugoslavs were sent off, too, leaving Willie Young to score the goal that put Arsenal through.

Red Star Belgrade did just enough to carry a 1–0 lead to their second leg encounter at Highbury. Alan Sunderland cracked the Yugoslav's powerful defence to give Arsenal hope; but Savic popped up to equalise and clinch victory for the visitors.

The Five Minute Final

Terry Neill added the name of £400,000 Brian Talbot to his squad for the Gunners' assault on the F.A. Cup. The former Ipswich midfield expert rewarded Arsenal with a goal in their Cup defeat of Notts County.

His industry and enterprise, admired from the Wembley bench by Neill the previous year, was a significant factor in Arsenal reaching their second successive F.A. Cup Final.

Talbot, proving an inspired buy, and Stapleton gave Arsenal what looked like an unassailable 2–0 lead; but with only five minutes remaining United drew level through Gordon McQueen and Sammy McIlroy.

66

United cheers had hardly died when Liam Brady stole away on a long penetrating run before slipping the ball to Graham Rix. Seconds later, Sunderland was slicing through United's defence to meet Rix's cross for the winning goal with seconds to spare.

European Cup Winners' Cup
The Championship campaign of 1979–80 turned into a duel between Liverpool and Manchester United. Arsenal's interest in silverware was confined to the F.A. Cup and the European Cup Winners' Cup, where they sank Fenerbahce and Magdeburg without too much trouble in the first two rounds.

Gothenburg were overpowered 5–0 to make the second leg a formality, but now came the most severe test of Terry Neill's early years.

The semi-final draw paired them with hot favourites Juventus, who won few friends in the first leg at Highbury with their aggressive tackling. Roberto Bettega, their World Cup striker, crippled David O'Leary, but justice was seen to be done when he conceded an own goal, the game ending 1–1.

No one gave Arsenal a chance in the second-leg in Turin, but such are the vagaries of football that an unknown Arsenal reserve was to see them into the Final against Valencia.

Paul Vaessen, plucked from the second team, scored two minutes from the end to put Arsenal through. Instantly a hero, Paul was not to know that in less than two years time his footballing career would be over, ruined by a knee injury.

67

He was not in Arsenal's line-up for the European Cup Winners' Cup Final in Brussels on 14 May 1980.

The Valencia team contained the West German Rainer Bonhof and Argentina's World Cup hero Mario Kempes.

Kempes hardly got a kick against Irishman David O'Leary and at the end of extra time the score read: Arsenal 0, Valencia 0.

Quite what Herbert Chapman would have made of the penalty shoot-out to decide the destiny of the trophy is beyond comprehension. Kempes and Brady, cold-eyed and deadly, both missed from the spot, but Valencia led 5–4 when Graham Rix stepped up.

Goalkeeper Pereira, moving for all the Arsenal kicks before they had been propelled, moved yet again to deny poor Rix, who went to the dressing-room in tears after Arsenal had come so close to winning their second European trophy.

It was their second major disappointment that month, for Arsenal had been beaten by West Ham in the F.A. Cup Final four days earlier.

Arsenal finished the season playing 70 matches, a record for an English club.

Neill for the chop
Liam Brady left for Juventus and Frank Stapleton took his considerable goal-scoring talents to Manchester United.

The loss of those two players was to lead to a barren spell for Arsenal in which Denis Hill-Wood, the most influential man in the boardroom after the War, died suddenly in 1982.

Terry Neill, well respected in his early days as boss, lost his way. That old sickness 'dressing room unrest' reared its ugly head again.

Neill splashed out £750,000 on Charlie Nicholas in June 1983 to appease his enemies, but by now they were sharpening their knives.

The 1983–84 season was to be his last in charge. Walsall, whose Cup giant-killing feat of yester-year had continued to haunt Highbury, did it again, beating Arsenal 2–1 in the Milk Cup fourth round before 22,000 dispirited Highbury fans.

There was no way back for Neill. Nine days before Christmas he was sacked. Don Howe was given control of the team on a trial basis.

In a scathing attack on his players, Neill observed: 'They don't seem to know what it is to hunger for goals and glory. On days like today I just think they want to pick up their money and go home.'

His critics argued that despite spending almost £8 million on players, Neill did not bring the success to Arsenal that his predecessor, Bertie Mee, had achieved for a lot less money.

However, history will record that Terry Neill did pretty well for Arsenal, both as a player and as manager.

Chapter Six

Gunners Blast Back

Don Howe, recognised throughout the game as one of England's finest coaches, was given the job of running Arsenal after Terry Neill's exit.

His talents on the training ground are well respected. The big question facing a cautious Highbury board of directors was: Can Don manage?

This concern was reflected in Chairman Peter Hill-Wood's announcement that Don Howe would be on trial for the rest of the 1983–84 season.

If there was scepticism in the boardroom, it is worth noting the attitude of the players, notably the colourful and controversial Scot Charlie Nicholas.

'Don is the number one. There's no one to beat Don as a coach in my eyes. He's not charismatic but that doesn't matter because he is so good at his job. However, if he could sell himself a little better, it might help him to fend off some of the unfair criticism.'

Praise indeed from the dressing-room that Howe inherited when he invited Raphael Meade to lead the Arsenal attack for the first time in a full game on 17 December 1983. Meade responded with a hat-trick against Watford. By Boxing Day he had cracked five goals in two games, starring in Arsenal's 4–2 win at Tottenham.

Charlie Nicholas, the wayward star already dubbed 'Champagne Charlie', contributed two goals in that game. His problems under Terry Neill's management might disperse under Howe's control.

He revealed later that Howe was a lot 'harder' on players than Neill had been in his term of office.

An uneventful era

England striker Paul Mariner was one of Howe's first signings in a £150,000 deal with Ipswich Town in February 1984. The following month Mariner scored two of Arsenal's four goals against his old club.

Howe was to be cursed by the same problem in his two-and-a-half year reign that Neill suffered. The club had no one with the appetite and ability to score goals like Liverpool's Ian Rush or Leicester's fast-rising star Gary Lineker.

Tony Woodcock, a regular in the England squad at the time, scored only 67 goals in 169 appearances for Arsenal. Charlie Nicholas, upon whom so much depended following his £750,000 move from Celtic in June 1983, just could not recover the golden touch that had carved 51 goals in his last season in Scotland.

Meade flattered to deceive on that glorious début day and it did not need an expert to form the opinion that Arsenal had never properly replaced the sadly departed, and often lamented, Liam Brady and Frank Stapleton.

Arsenal came no higher than sixth in the League in Howe's three seasons, though spirits were certainly high when Arsenal beat Liverpool 3–1 in the League on 8 September 1984. They went to the top of the First Division for the first time since February 1972.

Around that time Pat Jennings celebrated his 750th League game by saving Ken Hibbitt's penalty for Coventry. At the end of 1984–85, this loyal servant was given a free transfer. Steve Williams, highly skilled but disturbingly temperamental, arrived for £600,000 from Southampton in December 1984, but not long after his début Charlie Nicholas was discussing his future with Don Howe, his house festooned in lurid newspaper cuttings of an alleged wild life beyond the disciplines of the Arsenal training ground.

Bonny Prince Charlie, darling of the North Bank but infuriatingly inconsistent for Howe, found his shooting boots in 1985–86. He scored eight goals in Arsenal's progress to the fifth round of the Milk Cup and the F.A. Cup. He scored 10 more in the League, but it was 'too little, too late' to save Don Howe's neck.

Don Howe's departure

After the Gunners' 3–1 win against Coventry at Highbury in March 1986, Don Howe shook Highbury by asking to be released from his contract. His snap decision was related to disclosures that the Arsenal board had approached Barcelona's manager Terry Venables, a man widely respected by Arsenal officials. It was a mucky business all round, clearly unworthy of the great traditions of the Highbury boardroom.

Howe left a proud legacy of achievement in an unusual form for a departing manager. Many of the youngsters the caring Howe had nurtured on the training ground were beginning to blossom. Sadly, they were not quite ready for their First Division baptism when his time ran out at Highbury.

Graham in the hot seat

Arsenal failed to tempt Venables to the Highbury hot-seat despite his greatly publicised trip from Barcelona to hear what they had to say. They turned instead to George Graham, a leading figure in the Double-winning side of 1971.

His calm, disciplined, authoritative, ambitious approach to the game as manager of Millwall and his dislike of anything unprofessional, in attitude or dress, was greatly admired by Hill-Wood's board. They got their man on 14 May 1986.

He said he needed time to assess the staff and he flatly refused to buy players until he knew they were good enough. Indeed, he didn't make his first big signing for months, until the end of the 1986–87 season when he plunged into the transfer market for Leicester's striker Alan Smith.

No one knew better than Graham that stories circulating in the capital about the private lives of some players were not all rubbish. He simply adopted the Liverpool principle of choosing players on merit, irrespective of their star quality.

It meant that Charlie Nicholas, perhaps the biggest name at Highbury, would not be guaranteed a place.

Graham gave the impetuous Steve Williams a midfield role that brought the best from the former Saint and England player. He blooded Tony Adams in a central defensive partnership with the revived David O'Leary.

Viv Anderson and England left-back Kenny Sansom formed one of the best full-back partnerships in the League.

Big Dubliner Niall Quinn came into the team alongside Nicholas, and youngsters David Rocastle and Martin Hayes were given extensive runs in a first season that was to restore Arsenal to their form of the seventies.

By Christmas 1986 Arsenal had lost only three League games. Their form dipped badly in March but they still managed to come a creditable fourth in the League.

They went 22 games that season undefeated, a club record.

Centenary celebrations
Arsenal became fierce cup-fighters that season. Huddersfield, Manchester City, Charlton, and Nottingham Forest had all been knocked over by the Gunners in the Littlewoods Cup (formerly Milk Cup) by the time they met Spurs in the semi-finals.

Crippled by injury in the first-leg, Arsenal were sunk by a Clive Allen goal. He scored again in the second-leg, but Niall Quinn, still not truly accepted, made a goal for Viv Anderson and scored a second one for himself, thus forcing a third meeting between the clubs.

Clive Allen again opened the scoring, but this goal-lust was to prove a sad omen for Spurs. First Ian Allinson and then the rapidly improving David Rocastle shot Arsenal to a Wembley meet-

Kenny Sansom (left), captain of the Arsenal team that defeated Liverpool to win the 1987 Littlewoods Cup.

ing with Liverpool, who held the trophy in an armlock after winning it four times in a row in the eighties.

Ian Rush opened the scoring, and the Press reflected that whenever the Anfield striker scores, Liverpool never lose.

Now Charlie Nicholas emerged from insignificance to play his finest game for Arsenal.

He scored on the stroke of half-time, and as Arsenal piled on the pressure against a strangely subdued Liverpool, he moved in for the kill seven minutes from time.

Perry Groves, carrot-haired and extremely fast, raced down the left touchline past bewildered Liverpool defenders before crossing to the lurking Nicholas. He mis-hit his shot, but the Liverpool goalkeeper had no chance in saving the ball. It took a wicked deflection to give Arsenal the trophy.

Arsenal had won the Littlewoods Cup in their Centenary Year!

Kenny Sansom, the captain, said afterwards: 'I wasn't bothered about the medal, I wanted the Cup. As a kid I had watched on television as people like Emlyn Hughes lifted the cups for Liverpool and his face told the same story of happiness. This is what I wanted.'

Tony Adams, the most improved defender in the country, was named the Professional Footballers' Association's Young Player of the Year.

Consolidating success
Meanwhile, Arsenal's manager had already strengthened his side for the 1987–88 campaign by signing Alan Smith, the free-scoring Leicester

striker, for £750,000.

He was allowed to remain at Filbert Street until the end of the season but his arrival placed a question mark over the future of Charlie Nicholas.

The 1987–88 season was to represent a campaign in which the club consolidated its good start under George Graham. They were not to enjoy the spectacular success of the previous year, but it saw them reach their second successive Littlewoods Cup Final.

This time they faced what, on the surface, represented less formidable opposition than Liverpool in the shape of Luton Town.

This time, the last-gasp winner was not to be scored by Arsenal but by Luton.

Brian Stein, scorer of Luton's opening goal after 13 minutes, sank Arsenal in the last minute.

In between the former England man's strikes, Martin Hayes and Alan Smith punctured the Luton defence, but Danny Wilson's equaliser in the 81st minute turned the tables before Stein popped up again.

History showed that some of Arsenal's most celebrated teams had known what it was like to suffer defeat when they were favoured to win.

Yet there was a feeling of undisguised optimism in the air with the 1988–89 season roaring into life after the European Championships.

George Graham has put the mighty Gunners' back where they belonged – in the driving seat for an assault on all the major trophies.

You can almost sense the nod of approval from the Great Man himself, Herbert Chapman.

Chapter Seven

Golden Greats

Alex James

His baggy shorts hung limply below his knees. His short, sturdy frame would go unnoticed on a pavement of shoppers. But Alex James was a giant on the football pitch.

He was born in the same Scottish village of Bellshill that bred two other greats, Hughie Gallacher and Matt Busby. Alex James, of Preston, Arsenal and Scotland would command a transfer fee of at least £2 million in today's market.

He was a magician with a football at his command. His wizardry tormented the toughest defenders, who often resorted to fouling the little Scot as his cunning left them leaden-footed.

He could pass a player with the ease of a snake sliding past a snail, and his accuracy in passing the ball over short or long distances from midfield made him kingpin of the famous Arsenal teams of the 1930s.

He launched his dazzling career in the white shirt of Preston North End, but it was as a member of Scotland's 'Wembley Wizards', who trounced England 5–1 in 1928, that James' career reached its zenith.

The Arsenal manager Herbert Chapman saw that Wembley game and went on a personal crusade to sign Alex James. He achieved his objective in the summer of 1929, when he wrote a cheque for a mere £8000 to pull off the bargain of the decade.

James scored one of Arsenal's winning goals in the 1930 F.A. Cup Final victory over Huddersfield, and won his second Wembley medal in the Gunners' team that beat Sheffield United in the 1936 Final.

Only the Scotland selectors of that era will know why they picked him for just eight international appearances between 1926–33.

In Arsenal eyes, Alex James was a genius.

Ted Drake

Few players have generated more electric excitement in their Arsenal careers than Ted Drake.

He was the complete centre-forward of his era. Tall, strong, and quick, he had a fierce shot and an unerring eye for a half chance.

He became one of the First Division's most heavily marked strikers after an astonishing performance for Arsenal against Aston Villa on 14 December 1935.

Despite a knee injury, Ted had nine shots at the Villa goal and managed to score seven times! He had a hat-trick by half-time, a double hat-trick on the hour, and with Arsenal's last attack he scored his seventh to create a First Division record that has stood ever since.

His blood and thunder style, fearless but fair, made him a nightmare to mark throughout his Arsenal career from 1934–39.

Ted Drake – scored 7 goals against Aston Villa in 1935.

He was a member of Arsenal's Championship winning teams of 1933–34, 1935–36, and 1937–38; but he will be remembered best by Gunners' fans of that era for scoring Arsenal's winning goal in the 1936 F.A. Cup Final.

Cliff Bastin sent Drake on a long run at the Sheffield United defence. The big centre-forward side-stepped United's captain Tom Johnson, and before the goalkeeper could move he had thundered a left-footed winner.

He averaged a goal in almost every game he played for Arsenal, wearing the number nine shirt at Highbury for five years after leaving Southampton.

He cracked 124 goals in 168 League appearances, and a further 12 in 14 F.A. Cup-ties, but made only five England appearances between 1935–38.

He moved into management after the war and is now a well respected ambassador for football in retirement from the game.

Liam Brady

Dublin born Liam Brady was the playmaker of Arsenal's highly successful teams of the 1970s.

Never the most enthusiastic Gunner on the training ground, he was certainly one of the great crowd pleasers in the Arsenal side from 1973–80.

He used his left foot like a wand to propel the ball from the left touchline to the right with laser-beam accuracy.

In a flat sprint he could never match some of the 'greyhounds' of the First Division, but in a 10 metre burst he could leave a defender for dead before unleashing a shot into the net.

His left foot shooting could be deadly from anywhere within a 30 yard range of goal.

He grew up in the same city that produced two other Arsenal stalwarts of his era, Frank Stapleton and David O'Leary.

He made 10 appearances in the 1973–74 season, but by 1974–75 had established himself in the Arsenal team.

He was a member of Arsenal's 1979 F.A. Cup winning team against Manchester United, and picked up a loser's medal in the 1978 and 1980 Cup Finals against Ipswich Town and West Ham.

He crowned an outstanding Arsenal career by steering the club to the European Cup Winners' Cup Final in 1980, but his last appearance for the Gunners was marred by defeat. Locked at 0–0 with Valencia after extra-time, Arsenal lost the penalty shoot-out 5–4.

Brady's glittering career took him to Juventus, Sampdoria, Internazionale, and Ascoli before he made a welcome return to London in 1986–87 when he joined West Ham.

He launched an outstanding career for the Republic of Ireland in 1975 and was still in the squad when Jack Charlton led Eire to the European Championships in the summer of 1988.

Arsenal's slump at the beginning of the 1980s is put down to Brady's departure to Italy, after making 307 appearances with a surprising tally of 59 goals from midfield.

Malcolm Macdonald

No player to pull on an Arsenal shirt was more popular with the North Bank supporters than Malcolm Macdonald.

He arrived in a blaze of publicity in 1976 and continued to make big headlines throughout his four year career at Highbury.

Frank, fearless and often outspoken, this colourful striker became known to his supporters as 'Supermac'. To his enemies, of which there were few, he was known as 'Supermouth'.

Big, powerful, fearless and possessing burning acceleration to carry him past defenders – he was the fastest player on the Arsenal books – Macdonald chose Arsenal instead of Spurs when Terry Neill signed him for £333,333.

His explosive shooting was to wreak havoc on First Division defences from the moment he arrived on the big scene as a Newcastle player. He headed the First Division scoring charts for the Magpies in 1974–75 when he blazed 21 League goals. He weighed in with 19 League strikes the following season, and in 1976–77, his first season at Highbury, he cracked another 25 First Division goals.

He boasted he would score 30 goals in his first season at Highbury. He was one short in League and Cup competitions, managing a creditable 29.

Supermac's England career was no less eventful. He strung together 14 England outings from 1972–76 without truly fulfilling himself at that level.

He reserved his finest England performance for a cool April night in 1975 when he single-handedly destroyed Cyprus by scoring all five England goals.

Osteo-arthritis of the knee joint forced Supermac into premature retirement in August 1979 at the age of 29.

Typical of Macdonald, he never expressed any bitterness about his crippling condition, and moved happily into management at Fulham after making just over 100 League and Cup appearances for the Gunners.

Pat Jennings

Arsenal's Northern Ireland international goal-keeper Pat Jennings became one of the world's greatest players in a brilliant career lasting more than 20 golden years.

Big Pat, born in Newry, County Down, launched his career with Watford in the 1962–63 season. Goalkeeping of his quality could not remain in the lower Divisions for long, and in 1964 he joined Spurs. He went on to make almost 500 appearances for the great North London club and to establish himself as one of the world's great goalkeepers.

He joined Arsenal in 1977 when some people thought his agility and safe-handling in the penalty area were falling into sharp decline.

How wrong they were. He performed marvels for Arsenal for a further eight years.

The Professional Footballers' Association honoured Pat in 1972–73 by making him only the third goalkeeper to receive their coveted Player of the Year award.

His command of penalty boxes was one of the great sights of football. He thought nothing of soaring high above a couple of muscular, bulldozing strikers to snaffle the ball from their heads

His favourite trick was to catch the ball one-handed!

Pat Jennings, who played in Arsenal's F.A. Cup Final teams of 1978, 79 and 80.

He played in Arsenal's three F.A. Cup Final sides of 1978, 1979 and 1980, collecting a winner's medal in 1979 to add to all the other trophies he had obtained in a glittering career.

By the time he retired at the end of the 1984–85 season, Jennings had made more than 300 League and Cup appearances for the Gunners.

But if his League record was remarkable, his history at international level was even more incredible. He played his first game for Northern Ireland in 1964 as a raw, untried Watford goalkeeper.

Twenty-two years later, at the 1986 World Cup Finals, he brought his career to a shattering climax by making his 119th and final appearance for his beloved country, a record number of international caps for a British player.

Pat Jennings, a six footer, will be remembered as the gentle giant, who also happened to be just about the best goalkeeper in the world for more than two decades.

Charlie Nicholas

Charlie Nicholas rose from kicking a tennis ball in the backstreets of Glasgow to become the darling of Arsenal's North Bank section.

Colourful, controversial, superb, and infuriating, Bonnie Prince Charlie was capable of wild extremes in four sensational years as an Arsenal player.

He jumped at the chance to join Arsenal when the Gunners' offered £650,000 for his brilliant goal-scoring talents in June 1983.

Arsenal beat off Manchester United and Liverpool when it became known that Charlie was prepared to leave Celtic, after scoring 51 goals in all competitions for the famous Scottish League club in the 1982–83 season.

His impact on arrival at Highbury was astonishing. The Arsenal fans had had little to cheer when Charlie made his début in the 1983–84 season, but after a few matches the club were receiving the bumper attendances they had enjoyed a few years earlier.

Charlie packed them in, but the goal-scoring touch that had made him a constant source of danger to Scotland's Premier Division defences eluded the Scot for much of his Arsenal career.

His strike rate at Celtic had been a goal every other game. At Arsenal he managed only 34 in his 148 appearances between 1983–87. In 1987 he was transferred to Aberdeen.

Charlie, born in Glasgow on 30 December 1961, fashioned his mesmerising control of a football in the street matches he played in Glasgow as a youngster.

His impudent skills were seen at their best in the 1987 Littlewoods Cup Final at Wembley, where Charlie Nicholas produced a champagne performance to score the two Arsenal goals that sent Liverpool crashing.

It was his final appearance for Arsenal in a chequered career at Highbury that had never been truly fulfilled.

Both at League level and at international level, where he has made intermittent appearances for Scotland since 1983, the great entertainer with all the tricks has a lot to do to achieve the levels of performance that his skills promised in his early Celtic days.

But when it comes to popularity, to the ability to add thousands to the gate, and the ability to produce the unexpected, Charlie Nicholas has few peers. The game desperately needs characters like him.

David O'Leary
The Rolls-Royce of First Division defenders, David O'Leary is cast from the same mould as Liverpool's captain Alan Hansen.

He has been first choice central defender at Highbury since making his début more than 600 appearances ago in 1975.

Born in London in May 1958, but brought up in Dublin, O'Leary signed as an apprentice with Arsenal in June 1973 and made his League début against Burnley in August 1975.

Only 17 when he became a first-team regular, his cultured defensive skills gained him recognition from the Republic of Ireland in 1977 when he made his début against England. By the start of the 1987–88 season, he had made 40 appearances for his country.

Surprisingly, O'Leary was omitted from the Eire team at the beginning of Jack Charlton's managerial reign; but he was clearly enjoying a renaissance to his career when new Arsenal manager George Graham insisted O'Leary was a major part of his plans.

The likeable O'Leary became arguably Arsenal's most consistent player in their three great F.A. Cup campaigns in 1978, 1979, and 1980.

He lost confidence and form through injury during the Arsenal slump of the early eighties;

but throughout the Gunners' Littlewoods Cup winning season of 1986–87, he was back to his best in a fruitful central pairing with the highly promising new England defender Tony Adams.

The fastest player on Arsenal's books, he is the Gunners' longest serving player.

Kenny Sansom

An ever-present in the England team since 1979, Kenny Sansom has developed into one of the world's best left-backs.

Few wingers have ever roasted Kenny either at First Division level or in the two World Cups he has played for his country.

Only 5ft 6ins tall, his tackling is strong and his recovery amazingly sharp if a winger is ever lucky enough to slip one of his snapping tackles.

He likes nothing better than to abandon defensive duties for a long run into enemy territory in the hope of getting a pop at goal. He admits that his goal-scoring record should have been better, but the Arsenal supporters have lost count of the dozens of goals he has made for his colleagues.

Born in Camberwell on 26 September 1958, Sansom was soon spotted by Crystal Palace scouts and persuaded to join the Selhurst Park club as an apprentice.

He made his League début for them against Tranmere in May 1975 and went on to play 172 League games before his outstanding progress caught the eye of the big clubs.

Arsenal snapped him up in August 1980 in an £800,000 exchange deal involving Clive Allen and Paul Barron.

He went on to captain the Arsenal team that won the Littlewoods Cup in 1987 by defeating the mighty Liverpool 2–1.

King Kenny said afterwards: 'I couldn't wait to get up those stairs and get my hands on the trophy. I wasn't bothered about the medal, I wanted the cup.'

Surprisingly, it was the first trophy the England defender had won in a career spanning more than 500 matches at League level.

On checking the Arsenal staff after his arrival as Arsenal manager, George Graham said of Kenny Sansom: 'Here is one of football's best players, someone with great standing in the game.'

That sunny smile, those biting tackles and penetrating runs with the ball glued to his toe-caps will linger long in the memories of Arsenal fans who have been fortunate enough to watch Kenny Sansom in a glittering career at Highbury.

Tony Adams
Every so often a huge talent arrives on the First Division scene that breaks all the rules governing the normal progress of a young professional.

Tony Adams, born in London on 10 October 1966, brought these credentials to Arsenal when he made his début for the club as a raw 17-year-old defender in November 1983.

A product of Arsenal's youth system, Tony smashed all the barriers to win his place in the first team as a regular central defensive partner for David O'Leary long before he celebrated his 20th birthday.

Phenomenal progress of that nature would surely be rewarded. It was, when Tony made his

Tony Adams, who joined the first team before he was 20.

début for the full England team in their 4–2 mass-acre of Spain in Madrid in February 1987.

And in the summer of 1988 he lifted his hugely successful young career on to another plane when he travelled to West Germany as a member of England's European Championship squad.

Tony Adams has been, literally, head and shoulders above his contemporaries since becoming an Arsenal first teamer in the 1986–87 season.

Tall, strong in the air, powerful in the tackle, and with a positional understanding way beyond his tender years, he has been marked down as a future England captain.

He has taken naturally to captaincy, barking instructions at his team-mates as if he, not they, have been around for years. Above all, he commands respect.

His competitiveness and head for the big occasion was given full reign when he stood up to withering pressure from the Liverpool attack to help steer Arsenal to victory in the 1987 Littlewoods Cup Final at Wembley.

Arsenal's history is littered with stories of players who blossomed at youth level but failed to go all the way. Tony Adams clearly does not fit into that category.

At the end of the 1986–87 season, he received the ultimate reward for his startling progress when the Professional Footballers' Association voted him Young Player of the Year.

David Rocastle
David Rocastle is part of a new generation of black footballers who have starred in the First Division.

Arsenal are particularly fortunate to field three of the most enterprising black stars in the League – Rocastle, Paul Davis, and Mike Thomas.

Already an England Under-21 star, David is tipped to become an England regular by the time the national team begins to prepare for an assault on the World Cup in 1990.

Born in Lewisham, South London on 2 May, 1967, David is a product of the Arsenal youth system.

He made his League début against Newcastle in September 1985 and was a regular member of the Gunners' First Division and Littlewoods Cup-winning campaign in 1986–87.

His consistency is unrivalled as he burns a flare path down the right touchline to launch wave upon wave of Arsenal attacks. His ball control has been honed to perfection, and many a First Division left-back has been given a roasting by the young Gunner.

He is not afraid to shoot if he can see a gap between goalkeeper and net. His tremendous acceleration and unerring eye for the half chance makes him one of the First Division's most dangerous raiders; but he is chiefly employed as a playmaker of the Arsenal attack.

Nicknamed 'Rocky', he spoiled a hugely successful 1986–87 campaign by being sent off against Manchester United after tangling with Norman Whiteside.

But by the end of that season, his misdemeanour had been forgotten and he was named Arsenal's 'Player of the Year'.

Index